# Volume 9
# Decodable
# Reader

Mc
Graw
Hill
Education

Bothell, WA • Chicago, IL • Columbus, OH • New York, NY

# Contents

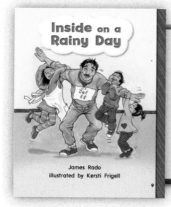

# The Rabbit Report

by Joanna Rice

illustrated by Brenda Johnson

Hello, readers. It's Robby Rabbit Reporter here. Welcome to The Rabbit Report. Today we will go in a tunnel. We will visit the unknown world of the common earthworm. We will talk to a real earthworm!

**Robby Rabbit:** I am under the ground at Earthworm Headquarters. I am chatting with Chief Earthworm, Ellen.

Ellen, please tell us what jobs you and your fellow worms do in the garden.

**Ellen**: So much happens here at our command center! You may not see us down in the dirt. But my worms do jobs that help plants grow.

**Ellen:** Do you know what happens to leaves and plants after they die? We eat them. But don't think it's a picnic for us. It is work! We clear space for plants to grow. We leave bits to make the soil rich.

**Ellen:** We are tunnel makers, too. Our tunnels create little spaces under the ground. The little spaces help water and air get into the soil.

**Robby Rabbit:** Tell us more, Ellen.

**Ellen:** Sure! We chew up leaves and trees. That makes the soil rich and helps prepare for new plants. Then little plants begin to grow.

**Robby Rabbit:** Ellen, this finishes our chat. We at The Rabbit Report want to thank you and the earthworms for helping plants grow.

**Ellen:** You can't replace a good worm. And we are always happy to help!

# Inside on a Rainy Day

James Rado

illustrated by Kersti Frigell

How would I describe my dad? He's the best! He can make anything and *do* anything. When it is rainy outside, he can keep us amused.

"I will amaze you with the fun we can have. It is time to be anything you want to be," he says.

Four chairs beside each other and a
blanket are useful for making a tunnel.

Dad takes turns driving us through.
He says that we need to explore
another land next.

It's time for a horseback ride. Two pillows under Dad's shirt become a saddle. My sisters have fun. We are hopeful that this horse won't start a stampede!

Last week, we helped Mom make homemade costumes for our puppets. Now, we are at a puppet show.

Dad said, "Last week's show was fine. This show will be finer still."

Now, it's time to travel by airplane!
We all decide to climb on board.

My sisters yell, "Go higher! Go faster!"

But instead, the ride gets bumpier and
bumpier! We all laugh. Dad is the best!

The airplane touches down for a landing. Mom is home.

"The excitement left me needing a nap," yawns Dad.

We frowned but Dad said, "Replace those with smiles. When I awake, we'll go an adventure of a lifetime!"

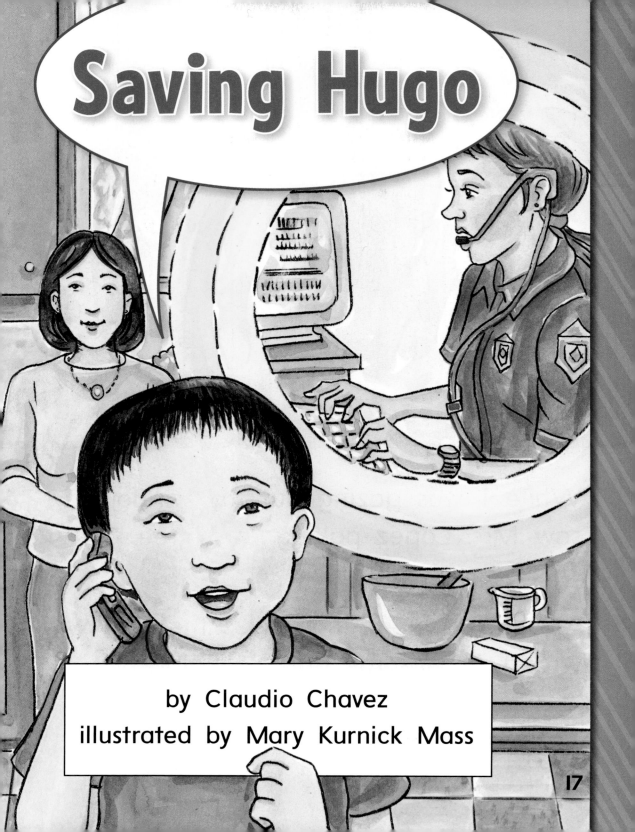

# Saving Hugo

by Claudio Chavez

illustrated by Mary Kurnick Mass

While I was gazing out my window, I saw Mrs. Lopez poking at a tree. She was using a big stick.

At that moment, I knew something was wrong. It was my duty to help!

I went out. There, beyond the leaves, was Hugo. He was silent.

"Hugo likes to see from the tree," said Mrs. Lopez. "But this branch is too high. He can be fearless but not now. He won't come down. He seems very afraid!"

"I have an idea," I told Mrs. Lopez. "I will call the local fire department. They will rescue him!"

"Thank you, Mason!" exclaimed Mrs. Lopez.

I returned home and told Mom about Hugo. I made the call.

A nice lady said, "Fire and Rescue. May I help you?"

"Yes," I replied. "A kitten is trapped in a tree! Can you rescue him?"

A few moments later, there was a loud siren. Then we saw a huge red fire truck. The truck stopped. Three firefighters jumped off the back.

"We were told there is a cute kitten that needs rescuing," one said.

"That's Hugo!" cried Mrs. Lopez. "He was silent before. Now he is mewing very loudly. He must be so scared up there on the highest branch."

"We'll rescue Hugo as fast as we can," replied the chief.

They used their tallest ladder. A few moments later, Hugo was rescued.

"I am so grateful," cried Mrs. Lopez.

"You're welcome," replied the chief. "Thank Mason for calling and for being so helpful. He is the real hero today."

# Paddle, Lucky, Paddle!

by Sinead Fallon
illustrated by Stephanie Pershing

Lucky was a little duck that lived in the middle of a big pond. She spent her days paddling back and forth in the blue water. When she needed rest, she waddled onto the sandy bank. Then she would think about her next meal.

One day, as she paddled across the pond, she began to think about bread. Could she bake bread? No, that was too much trouble! Could she go to the store for bread? No, she couldn't. Was there bread at home? No, there wasn't.

"There is no way to get bread," she grumbled. Her tummy grumbled, too.

28

There was talking and giggling coming from the bank. Lucky paddled over to see what was going on.

"A picnic!" she cried. "When people have picnics, they have bread to eat!"

She felt lucky indeed.

"I wish I was able to paddle faster,"
Lucky thought. "I'll wiggle and waggle
and see if that helps. I don't want the
people to gobble all the bread! All I
want is just a little nibble."

Lucky flapped her wings and quacked.

"Look!" a girl cried. "It's a little duck! It has travelled far to come see us. Let's give this duck a snack!"

Lucky paddled closer, hoping that the nice girl would give her a little bread.

"Here you go. This is a little sample!" the girl said as she gave Lucky some bread. "If you like it, I will get more."

"What total luck I've had to find this picnic today!" Lucky thought. She giggled as she gobbled the bread up!

# Saucy Sweetness

by Brian Diaz

illustrated by Kersti Frigell

One morning, Grandma Weaver decided she wanted to speak to her sweetest granddaughter, Joan.

"Hi, dear. It's Grandma Weaver. I am calling for a reason. Are you free today? I think it would be fun to cook a meal together."

"I would really enjoy that!" squealed Joan. "I'll make sure it's okay with Mom. If she agrees, I will see if she will give me a ride."

"I am delighted!" replied Grandma Weaver. "I am eager to see you soon."

Mom was happy to drop off Joan at Grandma Weaver's house. Joan ran to the door beaming. Grandma Weaver remembered Joan when she was just a baby. This girl is growing by leaps and bounds, Grandma realized.

Joan greeted Grandma Weaver.

"I couldn't wait to get here," she said.
She gave Grandma Weaver a really
big hug.

"You are the sweetest girl," Grandma
Weaver replied.

"What should we make?" Grandma Weaver asked. "We could make oatmeal cookies, raisin bread, breakfast bars, or even chicken stew."

"How about that sauce you make with tomatoes?" Joan asked. "Mom believes it is the best sauce in the world!"

"Being a good cook means reading the recipe carefully," Grandma Weaver explained. "You read the recipe and I will get out the containers and food."

"That's great," said Joan. "We should start with one teaspoon of sugar and three big tomatoes."

Joan couldn't wait to begin eating the tasty sauce. But for now, she would be satisfied with the smell of sweetness. It was coming from the steaming pot.

40

# A Perfect Job

by Ruth Brown
illustrated by Len Epstein

Benjamin looked in the mirror.

"Ben," he said to himself. "You are a just kid. But I know you can do something really different in life."

He was not interested in joining a circus. He was not that artistic. But he did not want just a normal job.

"I know!" he cried. "A firefighter is an exciting job. I will be a fearless firefighter. I will rush to places that are burning and put out the fire. It will be difficult but exciting."

But then Benjamin had another idea.

"An astronaut!" he cried. "An astronaut can discover new planets. I will introduce an important new planet to the entire world."

He couldn't wait to get into outer space!

Before Benjamin knew what was
happening, he found himself climbing
higher and higher up a tree!

"Help!" he cried.

Dad grabbed a ladder and got him.

"I think you might be safer on the
ground than outer space," Dad said.

"I know!" he cried. "What could be more perfect than a knight in shining armor? There is no one braver than a knight! I will face danger when I track down a fire-breathing dragon. I will defeat the dragon and return the stolen silver to the king. There could be no greater job than that!"

Benjamin raced through the house.

"There is the dragon now!" he cried.
"Have no fear, Dad! I will face this
monster and fetch the silver from his
jaws before it is too late!

"I think Patch needs to find a quieter
place to chew his bone," Dad said.

"Dad," Benjamin asked, "why are you dressed like that?"

"This morning you have been a firefighter, an astronaut, and a knight," Dad said. "So I have decided that I want to be YOU! I think that being a kid is better than being a dad!"

# Volume 9

**Decodable Words**
**Target Phonics Elements:** Closed Syllables
*begin, center, chatting, command, common, earthworm, Ellen, fellow, finishes, happens, happy, hello, picnic, Rabbit, Robby, tunnel, visit*

**High-Frequency Words**
**Review:** *are, into, of, our, sure, to, today, what, you*

**Story Words**
*earthworms, headquarters*

**Decodable Words**
**Target Phonics Elements:** Final -*e* Syllables
*airplane, amaze, awake, beside, decide, describe, explore, homemade, lifetime, outside, replace, stampede*

**High-Frequency Words**
**Review:** *another, anything, have, of, other, our, said, says, through, too, was, you*

**Story Words**
*adventure*

**Decodable Words**

**Target Phonics Element:** Vowel Team Syllables

*about, agrees, beaming, believes, breakfast, containers, cookies, couldn't, eager, eating, enjoy, explained, granddaughter, greeted, growing, oatmeal, okay, realized, reason, raisin, reading, really, replied, satisfied, saucy, sweetest, sweetness, teaspoon, tomatoes, Weaver*

**High-Frequency Words**

**Review:** *give, of, one, was, you*

**Story Words**

*recipe*

**Decodable Words**

**Target Phonics Elements:** *r*-Controlled Syllables

*armor, artistic, before, better, braver, burning, circus, danger, different, fearless, firefighter, greater, higher, important, interested, ladder, monster, morning, normal, quieter, outer, perfect, return, safer, silver*

**High-Frequency Words**

**Review:** *another, are, been, from, have, one, onto, said, through, to, was, you*

**Story Words**

*mirror, discover, idea*

## Decoding skills taught to date:

**Phonics:** Short *a*; Short *i*; Short *o*; Short *e*, Short *u*; *l*- Blends; *r*- Blends; *s* -Blends; end Blends; Long *a*: *a_e*; Long *i*: *i_e*; Long *o*: *o_e*; Long u: *u_e*; Soft *c*, Soft *g* ,*-dge*; Consonant Digraphs: *th, sh, -ng*; Consonant Digraphs: *ch, -tch, wh, ph*; Three-Letter Blends; Long *a*: *ai, ay*; Long *i*: *i, igh, ie, y*; Long *o*: *o, ow, oa, oe*; Long *e*: *e_e, ee, ea, e, ie*; Long *e*: *y, ey*; Long *u*: *u_e, ew, u, ue, /ûr/*: *er, ir, ur, or*; */är/ ar*; */ôr/ or, oar, ore*; */îr/ eer, ere, ear*; */âr/ are, air, ear, ere*; Long *a*: *a, ea, ei, ey*; Silent Letters: *wr, kn, gn, mb, sc*; Silent Letters: *rh, gh, bt, mn, lf, lk, st*; Diphthongs: *ou, ow*; Diphthongs: *oi, oy*; Variant Vowel: */ù/ oo, ou, u*; Variant Vowel: */ü/ oo, u, u_e, ew, ue, ui*; Variant Vowel: */ô/ a, aw, au, al*; Variant Vowel: */ô/ augh, ough*; Short Vowel Digraphs: */e/ea, /u/ou, /i/y*; Consonant Digraphs: */f/gh, /sh/ch, ss* Closed Syllables; Open Syllables; Final *e* Syllables; Consonant +*le* Syllables (+*le*, +*al*, +*el*); Vowel Team Syllables; *r*-Controlled Syllables

**Structural Analysis:** Plural Nouns *-s*; Inflectional Ending *-s*; Plural Nouns *-es;* Inflectional ending *-es*; Closed Syllables; Inflectional Ending *-ed;* Inflectional Ending *-ing*; Possessives (singular); Inflectional Endings *-ed, -ing* (drop finale *e*); Inflectional Endings *-ed, -ing* (double final consonant); CVCe Syllables; Prefixes *re-, un-, dis-*; Suffixes *-ful, -less*; Compound Words; Contractions with *'s, 're, 'll, 've*; Open Syllables; Contractions with *not (isn't, aren't, wasn't, weren't, hasn't, haven't, can't)*; Inflectional Endings and Plurals (change *y* to *i*); Comparative Inflectional endings *-er, -est*; Irregular Plurals; Abbreviations; *r*-Controlled Syllables; Plural Possessives, Prefixes *pre-, non-, mis-*; Consonant +*le* Syllables (+*le*, +*al*, +*el*); Contractions with *not (wouldn't, couldn't, shouldn't)*; Vowel Team Syllables, Suffixes *-y, -ly;* Comparatives *-er, -est* (with spelling changes); Three or More Syllable Words; Suffixes *-ness, -able, -ment, -ous*